Words of a Poetriot
By Latisha J.Greaves-Barker

A young woman's poetic journal on
life, love, God and growing-up

ISBN: 978-0-6151-7153-1

Dedicated

This book is dedicated to those who have ever made me laugh; who have ever made me cry; who have ever made me angry, sad, happy, surprise or glad. Those who chose to say goodbye. Those who have guided me and advised me, shared a bit of wisdom with me, to those whose strength, talent, wisdom, intellect, confidence and courage I admire. To those who share a passion for the arts with me. To those who have abused or misused me, discriminated against me, unjustly accused me, pre-judged me. Those who tried to fool me, refuse to school me, lied to me, and broke their promises to me. This book is for you and about you. For without you I would not have anything to write about. Without you I would not find the strength and courage to be who I am.

Also dedicated to:

My mommy, Annette F.George
My Dad, Sheldon
My bigger younger brother, Shane
My littlest little brother, Jonathon
My big little sister, Joliel
My other little sister, Arriel
My littlest little sister, Tatyanna
My husband, Kenneth
(Who made all my dreams come true)
and my precious jewel
Kytara Diamond

A Special note to my Step-mom and Step-dad Veronica and John

To mom-mom, I love you and miss you
(Ruby Gregg)

Thank you all for your love and support

Contents

Chapter Four: The Right One

Chapter Six: Under My Christmas Tree

Chapter Seven: The Sweetest Love

"For I know the plans I have for you,"
declares the Lord, "plans to prosper you
and not to harm you, plans to give you
hope and a future."

Jeremiah 29:11

Words of a Poetriot
By Latisha J.Greaves-Barker

Introduction

My poetic journey started out with a love
letter to a boyfriend; along the way I found
an art form which became my outlet for
self expression and discovery. Throughout
the last seven years of my life, I have
illustrated many emotions and
experiences in my poetry, joined and
quickly became coordinator of a literary
arts organization, published many of my
works in the local newspapers, started a
literary/performance arts group of my
own, and expanded my love for writing
into writing articles, which I put to good
use when publishing my own magazine.
Now all these experiences have become a
thing of the past and my life has taken a
different course, however I would like to
share some of the poems with you that I
wrote during this particular phase of my
life.

L.J.G.B

Chapter One
"Poems of love"

This Chapter talks about love in its many forms, love of poetry, love of family, love of God, love of nature, love of life, love of self.

Dear God

Thank you for inspiration
Thank you for education
Thank you for opportunity
For poetic unity, for a beautiful soul,
wonderful friends and family
Thank you for wisdom and strength, my
personality
Morality, honesty, integrity, my nationality
For creating me, giving birth to another
poet, lover of life with a passion for
creativity
Thank you for fighting with me the battle
of jealousy and envy
Thank you for spirituality, natural beauty
of the sea, the sand, the birds, the trees
for my abilities, for possibilities, for poetry
For beautiful, beautiful Barbados
For Life
Thank You
With love, your child, me

Ruby

We welcome you with open arms into
heaven's gate
For this precious jewel heaven's angels
have await,
To join us at God's dinner table to feast a
hearty feast
Rest my child for all is well, your soul
shall be at peace,
On earth you did your heavenly duties
Yes, you played your part
You cared for others more than yourself,
You loved with all your heart,
Come my child take my hand
Walk with me to the promise land,
Your thrown is set at your father's side
In God's Kingdom you now reside,
Forever and ever, eternally
Your memory will always be cherished by
Your friends and family,
The lives you've touched with God's sweet
kiss
In their hearts, you, they will dearly miss.

To God's precious jewel.

(To Mom-Mom) **R.I.P**

The Notebook

Each page blank
Till one day she
took it out of the store
Now, the question is
Did she find it?
Or did it find her?
Seem there relationship was meant to be
She filled its pages with many stories
Each day words are written on these pages
Words of love, words of hate
Words of sadness, words of pain
Words of gladness, words of joy
The ink
The ink that help tell these tales
Ink of life
A life created by God
A life designed specifically for the tasks
of sharing words
Words of wisdom
and this notebook
will stand the test of time

Good Morning Sunshine

A brand new morning
A brand new you
A brand new day
There are lots to do

A brand new hello
Another chance at life
Another morning to put up a good fight
Another opportunity to do it right

Thank you, Jesus
It's because of you
Another morning
To do what God ask me to do

Hallelujah
The sun is out

In Jesus name I've got to shout
Good Morning Sunshine
Welcome New Day

God's Blessings
I pray
I'm awake
I'm alive
Another chance to live

This day I say
I'll find my happiness
For no one, neither me
Knows what tomorrow brings

All I have is right now
To care for life
To care for me and my family
Good Morning Sunshine
Thanks for shining on me

This is for u

This is for u
The reason my very existence is true

This is for u
The epiphany of my soul

This is for u
The fulfillment of my heart

For u
Every breath I take
Every morn I wake
Every move I make

For u
The reason I prayer
The answers to my prayers
U

I smile at the thought of u
I cry in awe of u
I believe in all you do
U

This is for u
The star of my dreams
The apple of my eye
The reason I am who I am
A very part of me

The reason love's so real to me
Because of you I see
I am loved
I feel love
I know love
U

This poem I write
Recite, let it take
Flight tonight

And stop
Among the stars
Where it belongs
With u

My God
My Love
My Family
My Friends
My Heroes

This is for u

Pond

Where the sun is shining
The water is flowing
The flowers are growing
The fish are swimming
The bees are buzzing
The wind is blowing
The birds are chirping
My mind is free
My soul sings songs-a-many
And all is right with the world

Thank you God
Let's not forget
Life is precious

My Mother's Garden

A place of peace and serenity
A place where love flows frequently
A place of sunshine
A place of rain
A GARDEN
With flowers named
LATISHA, ARRIEL, TATYANA
& SHANE
A place of laughter
A place of tears
A place of comfort
A place of fears
My mother's Garden
A place where God's hand has touched
Where love, integrity, trust and joy
Is found so much

Strong Woman

I don't think I ever met a woman
Quite as strong as you
Woman you're a fighter
And I admire you

I have seen you survive so much
I would have certainly fallen apart
But you remain strong because of your
continued prayer
And the love inside your heart

Strong woman tell your story
So young people could look up to you
The world would not be where it is
If not for a woman like you

You fight for all your children
You fight to raise them right
Now my queen today
You have won your fight
Your children love you
Your husband too
You have a home full of joy and happiness
Because through it all you kept your faith
Now you have been bless

Mama

Sometimes you are miserable
Sometimes you make me so mad
I just want to scream and shout
Or hit something
But you are still incredible

My friends come and go from my life
My boys are here today and gone
tomorrow
But you are always here through my
happy times and sorrows

Sometimes my dad's around, sometimes
he's not
Rainfall sunshine you are by my side
In you I can confide

You don't smile as much as I would like
you to
But when you do the sun comes out, life is
brighter
The atmosphere is warmer

You are the star that guides me at night
You are the warmth and kindness that
makes life alright
Sometimes you say things that make me
worry about you
But my queen you don't know how much
your princess loves you

You've shown me strength in a way I could
never understand

You've showed me I am more
than....second hand
You've shown me faith in God above
His healing hand and precious love
You push me for the best, mom you are
the greatest

You are an angel God sent from above
For you I would give all my love
With the stars as my guide, write your
name in the sky
"World's Greatest Mom," words flying high

If I could fit each one of your fingers with
huge diamond rings
Buy you a limousine, a mansion and all
those rich people things
I'd magically make all your dreams come
true
All because I love you

Father

A leader, a teacher
A flashlight when the electricity goes out
The strength, the protector, the provider
The man with the power in his hands to
shape the world
In us
The thinker, the decision maker
The one who direct us to the right path
He is the example, the action, the words
He is wisdom
He rescues us when we are about to fall
He takes care of us all
He sticks around when the going get tough
Rest assure, he is with us
He speaks forceful when necessary
He is extraordinary
He's soft-spoken, he's tender, loving and
kind
He is strict when need be
He speaks the truth, he sets us free
Father is not a God, he is a man
He finds his wisdom with God on his right
hand
This is the definition of DAD

The Dynamic Duo (A poem for Shane)

If today I had a choice to choose my
partner in crime
Replace you, not even, never
Not today, not ever, not this time

We complete each other like Marc Anthony
and Cleopatra
Bonnie and Clyde, Yin and Yang, hand
and foot
We are nothing without each other

What good is a song without a voice?
What good is a problem without a choice?
I'm no good if you aren't there
I'm no good if you don't care
It breaks my heart when we fight
Like a wild animal trapped in a cage
That just isn't right

Sorry when I say I hate you,
Sorry when I call you names
But if you go tomorrow thinking it's true
Then my love would be in vain
The dynamic duo, that's who we are,
What's a racer without his car?
What's a biker without his noise?
What's a child without toys?

We are stronger banded together,
Than we could ever be apart
You are my friend, you are my brother
And you will always have a special place in
my heart

Beauty

A word that speaks for itself
When I think of the word beauty
I see the birds in the sky on a bright
sunny day

I see the soft sweet symphony Mother
Nature plays
I see the green in the trees and the ocean
blue
But best of all I see you

I see your heart so real, so true
I see your eyes, I see you
I see what you truly desire to be
And in my heart I know you see me

This Kiss

Gazing into your beautiful brown eyes
I knew you wanted to kiss me and
I wanted to kiss you

The closer you got to me
The deeper my breaths became
My body heat turned up ninety-eight
degrees

I touched your smooth skin, caressed your
body
You touched my smooth skin, caressed my
body

I never wanted you before as much as I
want you now
You placed your fingers between mine
I connected with you time after time

Your soft sexy lips touched mine
The butterflies in my stomach went wild
and crazy
I felt as I had released the tension I had
inside of me

You freed me and took all my troubles
away
This is so wrong but it feels so right
I wish it never had to end
I wish I didn't have to let you go

I never felt this way before
The way I feel tonight

Paint me a Picture

Paint me a picture
Where the trees are blue
And the sky is red
The birds are green
And the flowers are grey

Where colors can live
As free as the creatures
that roams the earth
None more significant than the other

Colors of the world
Collaborating as one
One heaven, one earth
One sky

Do not be blinded by colors
Nor do not consider one more
Important than the other

God made each pigment
With its' own beauty and texture
That makes us feel sad or happy
Angry or surprise

But as one
They just make us feel alive
So paint me a picture
of a colorful world

Unique

What makes us unique?
Do you ever wonder?
What makes us different?
I often ponder

Is it our hair, our eyes or the
 color of our skin?
Is it the clothes we wear or the
 house we live in?

What makes us stand out?
Stand out from the rest
Do you know the answer?
What do you suggest?

Is it the money in our pockets or
 the shoes in our closets?
Is it the earring in our ear or the
tattoo you wear?

Unique is a very interesting word
It is very rare in people
I've heard

In my opinion I don't think that's true
Cause we are all different
That's what makes you, you

Sometimes we like the same things
Sometimes we don't
Sometimes we'll fight
Sometimes we won't

It's our personality, our likes, dislikes
Our heart and soul
Our dreams and goals
That defines who we are
Not the size of our house and our type of
car

Chapter Two
"Words of a Poetriot"

This Chapter talks about art, poetry, words, expression, individuality and it reflects the heart of a poet.

What is a Poetriot?

A Poetriot is a poet/artist who stays true to his art/passion. This means an artist who has not sold out.

My Style

You paint a picture of man in solid form,
I use sticks where his hands should be

You paint in black and white
I use a collage of colors so bright

Again you write in dialect
Because that's your way, while I
Write in slang, doing it my way

You use the Queen's English
I make up my own language

I have my style and you have yours
Just because you don't get it or my way
does not suit you
Am I any less an artist, any less a poet?
Should I be appreciated less or respected
less
Do I have to conform to the standards set
by you?
You create limitations that I may not go
beyond?

Am I not worthy?
Because my style isn't yours
You know what, I think not
Not today

Today and until I meet my destiny
I'll keep on doing it my way

Words of a Poetriot

Pa pum, pa pum
My heart it beats
My mind it speaks

The twisted sound of aspirations
Float through my veins like intoxicating
emotions
Breaking to pieces my crisp devotions

Devoted to my secret
No I will not share it
Devoted to my words
Even though they are unheard

Falling to my page so naturally
Scrawling, scribbling sentences
Stripping off stress and strain from my
body
Breathing new life into my soul
And on to that notepad
That crumpled up, folded so neatly
I can take it anywhere notepad

My interpretation of yesterday
My vision of now
My premonitions of tomorrow

The complicated-simplified
Doctrines of just who I am
The purest alliteration of a poetic virgin

My pen is my weapon
My page my shield

My knowledge my compass
My faith in God my force field
Silence doesn't instigate
Lack of burning opinions
Needed to be expressed
It's just being reviewed
Before it takes its rest
On your ears

Constructive criticism
Can lead to creative destruction
Who are you to force your poetic rules
upon me?
What makes your vision more sacred than
the images I see?

It comes when it comes
And not before it's suppose to come
So who's to say when you've found that
perfect one?

Over-explanation needs to take a vacation
Forcing me on you, no
It should be your own interpretation

Standing silently still a naked newborn to
the earth
My birth

United as one we gather
In humble artistic form
None more valued than the other
We are poetriotic brothers
Dancers, singers, writers, photographers
Musicians

Man of the arts
Interpreted only as to be interpret

The Piece

God, please lay the words on my heart
The things I want to say
That I really can't in any other way
Than in a piece

Now this piece is absolutely about nothing
But it says everything about
All the things I want to say

Like who am I?
Who are you?
Are you real?
Whose reality is really reality?

Who can I trust?
Can I trust you?
Or should I trust no one
Who's virgin of the perfect piece?
Is really perfect
Do you have it right?
Do I have it wrong?

Is the real world real?
Or an illusion all along
Am I really a poet?
Or a poet who's really a painter
Mistaken for a photographer
Disguised as a storyteller

My piece has no structure
It doesn't make much sense
So should I stop writing?
Would that make the difference?

Not about politics, not about sex
Not on religion; who made me glad
Nor who made me vex

I'm not writing to make you feel good
Or make you feel blue
This is not about you

Does this fit the profile of how a piece
should be?
It's not on my favorite topic
Needless to say, that's me

It's not dedicated to mom
Not a poem for my dad
Not about the love I have now or the love I
had

Not about my pain, not about my sorrow
Not about when today becomes yesterday
Now suddenly it's tomorrow

I'm just writing this piece about nothing
Another piece of poetry
What do you know!
Another piece about nothing is done
Glad to get that off my chest
Now wasn't that fun

Words

This must be the hundredth time
I've tried to describe the indescribable
Satisfy the insatiable
Mention the unmentionable
Unsimplify the simple
That feeling I get
When life gets a hold of me
And things get good
Real good
Like taking a bus ride and getting a
glimpse of the sea
Like a smile on a man's face who is
winking at me
That's when the words hit me

This must be the thousandth time
I tried to describe the indescribable
Satisfy the insatiable
Mention the unmentionable
Unsimplify the simple
The words they hit me
They float through my tears
They wrestle through my fears
Artistically seeking
Poetically speaking
Trying to find me spiritually, mentally,
physically
Through my poetry
Once again I try to describe the destiny of
a poet

Just Write

Sometimes in life a writer needs to be free,
find that quiet spot
And count; one, two, three; breathe and
exhale, think, refresh, renew
Release all negative energy, revive and
redo

Cool down and take the time
Smell the roses, redefine
Look into your inner soul and see who you
really are
Listen to the music of your heart
Gaze on that shining star

Hear the words dancing in your head
Dream big dreams of tall mountains
And flowing streams

Be adventurous, explore your world
Be courageous, hug your earth
Let your imagination run wild and free
Live and just be

Under Construction

I still haven't found the perfect poem
that's gonna set it off yet, the older I get
my technique keeps changing
One minute I'm writing about red roses
and how sweet it is
Next thing I'm wishing for rain, going in
sane threatening to slit my wrist
People listen as my poem keeps unfolding,
listening intently waiting for my poem to
end, it has to have an ending, everything
does
But I haven't got a clue as to when
So I just keep writing cause
My words don't stop coming and my ink
never runs out
And I always always have something new
to write about
Life's just like that

 I still haven't found the perfect song to
escape my tongue
Nor the perfect dance to that perfect song
I am still paint strokes
Upon the canvas
For my life's a work of art
Still being sculpted into a masterpiece
How many days till its completion?
I do not know
For my life's the perfect poem still
Under construction

Chapter Three
"Metamorphosis"

This Chapter talks growing up,
imperfection, understanding,
change and dreaming big dreams.

Imperfection

Upon this lonely alter
I sadly sit
A place you've trapped me
Destined for invincibility
You've convinced me
Time after time
Flattered by your intensity
Your continually growing faith in me
You set impossible standards for me to
live up to
Leaving me confused in what I should do
You're not conceiving the inevitability
I am not perfect
And I never will be

Metamorphosis

What's this feeling taking over me?
What's this feeling in the depths of my
body?
Something's different, it's not the same
I can hear him calling,calling my name

Who or what is this calling to me?
Why is it so dark, too dark to see?
I long to feel the wind blowing in my
hair
I long to dive in the ocean over there

I long to smell the flowers and climb the
highest tree
What is this feeling coming over me?
Things are changing, it's not the same
I can hear him shouting, screaming my
name

Where is the girl I use to be?
Where is that girl, where is she?
Why is it so dark, so dark inside?
Stop, Listen
I hear him
I open my eyes

My love, my precious angel
He calls to me
My goddess, my queen, my Caribbean
beauty

I open my eyes
I step out of my cocoon
And I fly

Like a Ghost

I am walking like some kinda ghost
Walking into oblivion
And I am lost
Lost in space on earth
Does that make any sense?
Anyway, forget it

I am walking like some kinda ghost
Walking into oblivion
And I am lost
Lost here
Here, where?
Here
If I knew where
Then I wouldn't be lost would I?

I am walking like some kinda ghost
Transparent but a mystery
Clueless yet full of knowledge
Do you understand what I am saying?
Never mind, don't think about it

I am walking like some kinda ghost
And I am worthless
Yet valued more than gold
I am walking like some kinda ghost
To meet my inevitable doom
But I stand my ground

I am walking like some kinda ghost
And I am dizzy
I am spinning in circles but I am not
moving

I am walking like some kinda ghost
And I'm scared
But of what I fear
I do not know

I am walking like some
Kinda ghost
Walking through my twenties

Misunderstood

I am often perceived as confused
 like I don't know who I am
or what I am about

You see me and think because I am silent
I have nothing to talk about

You think instead of being true to me
I should be just like you

You act like because I don't do it your way
I don't know what to do

Newsflash
Get you bulletin board in check

You think you know how I should be
But no one knows better than me
Other than God

You think you've got me figured out
But you don't have a clue

If you really wanted to know me
Ask me
A little tip for you

Trippin'

Sometimes I wonder what's wrong with me
Sometimes I'm looking but just don't see
Sometimes I'm listening but just don't
hear
Sometimes I am doing but simply don't
care
Am I crazy, am I mad?
When I am upset I laugh like I am glad
When I'm happy I cry like I am sad
Am I trippin' because I tell the truth most
of the time
Or because I believe there's more good
than bad in mankind
Am I crazy, am I mad?
No guess I am just trippin'

Not the only one

I know I'm not the only one to lose myself
in a dream
I know I'm not the only one to dream
further than my eyes can see
And I know I'm not the only one to want
more than my skin can touch
My dreams are big and I want them so
much

Not all dreams are good and destined to be
But to tell me stop dreaming
Where does that leave me?
Restless nights of empty screens
An empty soul of madden screams

I maybe far fetch then again maybe not
But to ask me to quit before I reach the
top
Is an unfair request I simply must not
oblige
My destiny only I can decide
Who am I to become?
What's to become of me?
I must go ahead and set on my journey

Life is a painting
Life is a dance
So I must put on my dancing shoes
Set-up my canvas
And take a chance

Who says our dance must carry the same
steps?
Who says our canvas must display the
same specs?
If I sound strange and you don't
comprehend
I don't need an enemy but I could use a
friend
Its' okay we're different
Let's make a deal
Let's just be who we are
Let's just keep it real

My Body

Sensually arousing
Mysteriously appetizing
Inevitably belonging
Naturally intimidating

A prince, a handsome warrior
An ultimate survivor
It's meant to be touched
But by only one
The one, the prince destined to be king
In search of a queen

The one
Who values it more than all his earthly
treasures
For now he's seen it he has but one
treasure
It's meant to be explored but by only one
The explorer, the traveler
The one who'll study each hidden detail
Carefully, scientifically, seductively

It is meant to be discovered
But only truly discovered by one
It stands before him transparent
And he'll see the soul within
It's mine for now
But soon it will belong to him and only
him

My soldier, my warrior, my king will
deserve
Such a precious gift

Nothing

Queen:

A soul sista, a kind-hearted lover
Lover of peace, not of war
She'll adore her king
Take care of her king
For this queen's world
Is nothing without her king

King:

He is a warrior, the leader
The man who values the heart, the body
and the soul of his soul sista
No one values her more
Because this king knows
Without his Queen he is nothing

So, you wanna know what love is?

Pull up a chair
Sit down and listen
You got time
I have nothing
But time for you

When I'm done
You'll understand what love is
Love is patience
Its' trusting each other

If you fall down
Its' my hand
That will be pulling you up

If you're sick
Maybe in the hospital
Its' me who will be
By your side

If you tell a lame joke
I'll laugh
Or maybe tell you how lame you are

When you talk to me
You won't have to question
If I'm listening
Because I will be

I'll put you
And your feelings
Before myself
Cause love is sacrifice

Love is a lot of things
Its' being together
Missing each other when apart
It all comes from the heart

Its' a small gesture
That draws a smile
Its' sharing feelings,
Dreams, mistakes, dislike

Its' ups and downs
And turnarounds
But you know what
Love is hard to find

So if there's trouble in
the beautiful ocean
Known as love
Fight because love's worth it

The Absence of Love

They think I should hate you
Because you choose to be different
They think the choice you made
Makes you a sinner

I don't know maybe you are
Maybe you are not
Who am I to judge you?
Simple little me

How can I sit there and point out
the stick in your eye?
When I might have a log in mine

If you are a sinner
I will love you still
If you are a saint
I will love you still

For the absence of love
is far more sinful than who you are
And what you choose to do
It's not my place to be judgmental of you

Change

Is it that you've grown up too fast or my
paste is just too slow?
Is it that I never knew you or I wasn't
around to see you grow?
Every time I come back here, I wonder
why, as I feel our bond drift further and
further apart
I search for the you I knew a longtime ago
the one with that permanent fixture in my
heart
Seeing you again, it's like I'm meeting you
for the first time
As my heart searches to find a spot for the
new you and my mind tries to decide
whether or not I want to
My God, you've changed
But even though I have yet to get to know
the new you
I love you and that will never change
So whoever you become
So wherever you go, whether we drift
closer together or further apart
You'll always have a place in my heart

Karma

Enjoy it now, when you judge me and
think you know me
You tell people what you think you see in
me
Karma
Someone will judge you too
Someone will think they know you
When they really don't

Enjoy it now, when you think you own me
You think I'm your puppet in a puppet
show but you just don't know
Karma
Someone will think they own you someday
Maybe they will, what can I say?

Enjoy it now
When you talk about me behind my back
I really don't respect that
Karma
When you talk about me
There will be someone talking about you
too

Enjoy it now
When you hurt me or lie to me
That's just for now you see
because when the pain is done
Karma
It's your turn and I have won

Enjoy it now
Your cruel mischievous way

Karma
These things will catch up with you
someday

Chapter Four
"The Right One"

**This Chapter talks about
romance, desire, lust, heart-break,
sex, relationships, boys and
matters of the heart**

My Kinda Guy

Okay,
I'm a free spirit
So I need my space
You have to know
When I need that
And stay out of my face

Truth is....
I don't have time to lie
So keep it real with me
Tell me how you feel
Then you'll be my kinda guy

Damn
I love to dance
To get my party on
So when no one's around
Turn on some music
And let you and me get down

Got jokes?
I love to laugh and I sure as heaven love to
smile
If the world is on your shoulder
And you forgot how to have fun
Then forget it, you're not the one

But be serious
We have some work to do
Work with me
And I will work with you

Marry me

Get on up and put that ring on
You snooze; you lose
And I know I am a good woman
Don't cheat
Know what you've got at home
And come home to it

Time
I need your time
So keep your money
And come over here and give me that
honey

Good Woman

Boy, you wouldn't know a good woman
If she walk right up to you
And slap you in the face

A good woman is one who knows what
she's got
She knows you don't have to look like
Halle to be hot

A good woman does not define herself by
what she's wearing
but better yet when she wears it, it's a
reflection of how she's feeling

A good woman does not try to take a man
for all he's got
Nor does she pretend to be someone she's
not

A good woman knows she is only half the
plan
And she knows how to treat her man

A good woman's got your back through
thick or thin
And she gets under your skin

Makes your knees weak
Your heart beat
And you know from now on
All that you do is for her

But listen very carefully
A good woman can only survive
In the heart of a good man

And a good man is one who understands
how to love a
Good Woman

The Right One

Looking, Searching, Meeting, Talking
Dating, Kissing, Dancing, Hugging
Where are you?
 I need you
Come to me, seek me, and feel me
Love me
The way I love you
Don't mind them
The guys of today and yesterday
They are not you and never will be
They will never love me the way you will
They will never make me laugh the way
you will make me laugh
So where are you?
Who are you?
Come to me, seek me, feel me and love me

The One

I think about you all the time
I envision your likeness in my mind
The first time you see me, you'll know who
I am
When I first see you, I will know you
The one

The one who'll make my knees go weak,
the one all my life I seeked
You will be the most wonderful guy in the
world to me because inside your soul I will
see

Not just another disciple in a crew
You'll always be yourself, that's what I'll
like about you
You'll make me feel like a princess
And to me your secrets you will confess

You will make me laugh, sometimes make
me cry
But you'll always be my sweet guy
Your spirituality will be a part of me
You will always be beautiful to me

You will be truthful and loyal, you will love
strong
I'll dance with you all night long
To our favorite love song
To you my heart will always belong

You'll know when I need my space

You'll know when I need to see your
gorgeous face
You'll know when I need you to hold my
hand
Because you're the kind of man who
understands

You won't be ashamed to show you care
My life will be complete because you're
there
Until that time I'll be thinking of you
You'll be the one who'll make all my
dreams come true

Glow

Do you know?
God brought us together
And that's the reason we connected so
naturally
We were simply meant to be
This feeling I'm getting in the pit of my
stomach
What does it mean?
And why do my breaths get heavier when
you're near me
Why do I feel like I must be around you
24/7?
And when 24 meets 7
I crave for more
Wanting 25/8
And when you hang-up the phone
After confessing you miss me
And you're coming to see me
I can't wait
So I put on my favorite dress
Sprinkle two drops of Glow by J.Lo
And come to see you
I picked the J.Lo Glow because that's what
you do to me
You make me Glow from inside out
When I close my eyes
I see you
Your mystery and intrigue
Your respect and honesty
Your fuzzy hair, sexy lips
And damn that cologne you wear
Old Spice
Damn, Damn, Damn

That's nice
Why is it when you're not there
I still taste you the same as when we last
kiss
I'm taken to a cloud higher than nine
A cloud called heaven's bliss
Do you know?
God brought us together
And what is it about you that makes me
weak
Reveals you're the baby boy I seek
Makes me high
So intoxicatingly head over heals happy
I cry
Tears of laughter flow through my eye
Mr. Romantic
My feet start to shake
My soul ekes because I am so damn in
love
With you
And those things you make me do
Like
Write you a poem just like this
Put on the negligee
And slow dance to Marvin Gaye
All night long for you
You, you, you,
My people would ask me "What is it I see
in you."
They don't understand
You are a part of me
I can't let go
And when we touch it's clear
My whole life with you I'm going to share

Do you know God brought us together?
Together, together
You and me
That's forever
Baby

Someday

Sometimes you call
Sometimes you don't
Sometimes you will
Sometimes you won't

What's on your mind boo?
Please let me know
You got me confused
This is out of control

I don't know if you love me
But I love you
That's the problem
I don't know what to do

You don't call me as often as I'd wish
But when you're with me
That's all gibberish

What we have between us
I just don't have a clue
All I know is
I breathe, eat and sleep
Thinking of you

I get hurt a little when you don't do what
you should
But then I see your smile
And it's all understood

We belong together
I know this in my heart
You might not believe me

But I knew I loved you from the start

But until you're ready to stop playing
games
I'll just be your friend
You won't forget my name

Shorty, I love you
Someday, you will love me
My baby boo
Someday it will be me and you

Shorty

Shorty, I'm feeling you
Like chocolate flavored ice cream
Shorty, I love you
Like movie stars love to be seen

Shorty, when you touch me
My heart skips a beat
Shorty, what you doing to me
You pulling me in too deep

Shorty, why don't you come over
And give me a sweet kiss
Shorty, I don't know about you
But I am really feeling this

Shorty, I love your smile
I love your eyes
I love your hair
Shorty, you haven't a clue how much I
care

Shorty, I love you
I love to feel your touch
Shorty, I think I love you a little too much

Crazy

You call, you smile at me
You hold me sometimes
I know you're digging me
But it's like you are afraid to say it
Barely able to show it
I try to be patient
I try to play it cool
The truth is, the deal is
I am really digging you
I am afraid to get too close to you
Because you never tell me how you feel
I'm afraid to open my heart to you
Then the truth you'll never reveal
Sometimes I wonder
If I'm just another girl to you
Just another fling
I'm often afraid you won't call
But the phone always rings
Now you got me going crazy
Got me going out of my mind
If I open my heart to you and you to me
What will we find?
The question is
Will you hurt me?
Will I hurt you?
Who would hurt who
Giving in, giving it up
Is a risk we're both afraid to take
I hope we don't lose it
I hope we don't lose out
And make a huge mistake
Right now, you got me going crazy
Going crazy for you

Breathe into Me

I need you to hold me tonight
I need to feel as if everything is going to be
alright
I need to know your love is true
I need to be with you
You must know this heart you hold in
your soul
Is fragile
I need to know
Will you love me so?
Cause loving me will not be easy
There is so much to do
But I'll love you
I need you to breathe into me
Breathe new life into my soul
Everlasting love, eternal love
Hold me tight
I need to feel the warmth my insides feel
when I am in your embrace
I need to see you smile at me
When I look into your face
I need to hear you whisper my name
Like it belongs on your tongue
Breathe into me
New life
Sing me a brand new song

Keep it Simple Stupid

I don't need you to buy me a diamond ring
Or take me on a Cruise around the world
I just need your love
Your unfailing love
I just wanna be your girl

Hold me when I need to be held
I'm not asking much
Kiss me tenderly when I need those lips
I just wanna be touched

Listen to me
When I have to speak, because I wanna
talk to you
Talk to me, when you need to chat
I just wanna listen to you

Roses and dinner in a fancy restaurant
That doesn't mean much
Sit next to me, with some snacks and a
good movie
I just wanna feel free to be me

We don't have to have a night on the town
As long as I'm with you
Let's play
A little Marvin Gaye
I just wanna dance with you

I wanna be your lady till the end of time
I wanna put my freak on you, cause baby
you're all mine

I'm down for whatever because you're my
kind of brotha

I guarantee it's you and me
Now until forever

Let's do how we do
It's not about me
It's not about you
It's about us
Like Bonnie and Clyde
You and I will ride
And if we go down
We go down together

Poems

I have written quite
A few poems
Since I met you
Man,
I must really got it bad for you

We Share a Poem

"So, I heard you write poetry?"
he said
"Yeah, I do"
He smiles and responds
"Wow, that's amazing, I do too"
"Oh my God, really you do?"

I think I am falling in love with falling in
love with you
But I am a slave to Father Time that
reminds me constantly;
It's only been a week or two since I first
laid my eyes on you

When the harshness of reality moistens
my cheeks with the rough texture of lives
Injustices, you took my face into your soft
hands and caressed it,
You blew my tears of weariness away with
the power of your words
You wrote me a poem

"Latisha, no matter what happens, what
you do, where you go, what you try
I want you to remember I'll always be by
your side"

I know this might sound like another
cliché love scene in an old romance novel
Hidden in a school girl's crush
But it soothes me; it soothes me that in
the deepest core of my heart, I knew it
wasn't a lie

I froze my tears, cease to cry
I smiled and thought about when you hold
me
You hold me so tight as if you could insert
your heart into mine
And create one heart beat
You would

Not only that but more as if you could get
deep inside my soul
Where no man has ever dared journey,
you would pack up
Your gear, kiss your friends and family
Good-bye and come into me

You locked your fingers between mine so
tightly I couldn't escape your grasp, not
that I really wanted to anyway
Then you'd say to me,
"We were meant to be, look how they fit
perfectly"

He said,
I wanna know you; I wanna make you
happy, I wanna fall in love with you"
I know cliché, right?

"Sometimes I feel so invisible" I would
confess to him

"You're not invisible; sometimes you are
all I see"
Cliché, Cliché, Cliché

Do I make you happy? He asked me

I smiled and replied, "Yes, yes, yes you do"

"You're a princess, you know that?"
I said," I think you're amazing"

The next day I gazed into his warm eyes
and whispered into his ears,
Are you ready to write that poem?"

God, I wish it would rain

Mama always told me;
"Never rush love,
Love will come to you when you least
expect
And you will have to ask,
Is this real or is this just another
Cinderella-Snow White fairy-tale
When you stop looking, love will come"

So this is my story;
I looked into his only-God-could-have-
made-them-so-pure eyes
And I see that cozy cottage, bedrooms for
three
Me, him, the kids, the family
A kiss on the forehead, a peck on the
cheek
I took his warm body into mine

Imagining the night before
Silk sheets, Marvin Gaye
Dining with fine wine

Just when I thought I was being to clingy
And I try to back up-give the man some
space
I realize he's the one holding me
He's the one caressing my face

Now question after question
Linger in my head
Is this real, is he real
Is this God's earth angel

Really lying next to me in this bed

Woke up by his prayers and a kiss on the
cheek
"Honey, breakfast is ready"
looked into the mirror and the reflection I
see, somewhat seems different it doesn't
look like me
I look happy
Truly happy

Maybe it is me; maybe I am more than I
ever thought I could be with him
Warm morning sun; please return from
whence you came
Don't misunderstand, I love yah!

But God, I wish it would rain
So my body would get cold and he'll draw
me closer to him
"Don't worry, I'll keep you warm baby"
He'll hold me so tight I'll forget whose skin
is whose
We'll fall into romantic slumber and
just.......
Aaaaaahhhhh

The Possibility of

I'm in love
Mmm,mmm,mmm
Man he is so fine
And I'd do just about anything to make
him mine
It seem like just yesterday our eyes locked
We connected
And I was infected by the disease of love
I'm in love
Only God above can curse this love
I'm in love
With his smile, his hair
The way he drives his ride
The clothes he wears
And when we are holding hands
We'll shrike a pose
Cause we look good together, right?
I'm in love
Like I have been before
Yesterday, during today, after tomorrow
I'm in love
With the possibility
of the infinity
of his sexuality
That fires up the chemistry
That covers the air
As I inhale the beauty
of the possibility of
Who we are,
us combine
You and me
Cause we look good together
I'm in love with getting to know

You
I wanna show you I'm good for you
And you for me
The photogenic, picture-perfect two
You and me
us combine
I'm in love
With the possibility of love

I just wanna Dance

I pretty much spent my whole life dancing
alone
I would shake it, break it, groove it, move
it, jazz it, blues it
You name it

Once in a while, I'd find myself dancing in
a small group
Then sometimes a large one

Every now and then it's just me and
another son
They come and go
Some say I move too fast
Others say I move too slow

But I still boogie on
I dance to my own beat
Every change of the track led to different
moves

Sometimes I watch someone else move
and
Copy a step or two
But most of the time I create my own
moves

Sometimes some dance instructor would
think he earned the right to tell me how to
move

Sometimes I follow
Sometimes I lead

Sometimes I'd be applauded
Sometimes I'd fall, bruise and bleed
But I would still dance

Suddenly, he came to me
Another dancer, a handsome stranger
With his arched eyebrows and gorgeous
kissable lips
He held his hand out to me
"Shall we dance?"

We spoke while we dance
We spoke of beautiful things
Our souls connected
As if just us on the floor

Then just like that, he let me go
Said I was dancing too fast
He wanted to dance slow
Then he wanted to dance with me no-more

He left me alone on the floor
But I just could not move anymore
So I look for a corner
And there I went
Stayed a long while
Till a voice HE sent

"Yo, yo Tish, it's time to get up off your
butt and dance again, cause baby girl,
your song still playing,"

How many left the floor because there
song is through,
They can't dance but you could

So what are you gonna do?

So I danced my way back on the floor
And stepped
When the Deejay played a tune
I thought I couldn't groove to, I tried to
leave the floor again
He played the music louder, harder
And called my name again

"Girl, just dance"

So I tried to learn some new moves to
make it through that song, then I
discovered he was playing my song all
along

Can't be Friends

I can't even begin to describe
The feelings I felt
When we shared our first kiss
Our first conversation on the boardwalk
The first time we held hands
I felt a lover's bliss
Suddenly the world was okay
And I was free
There was not a soul on this earth
Except you and me
We moved really fast
Fell really hard
At least I did
I thought you did too
Now I'm not sure
What was really going on with you
The things you said, the way you held me
The entire beautification of us unfolded
naturally
Now today, months later
I'm still stunned by how it changed so
drastically
I felt love for the first time
And lost it before it even sank in
I dropped my stance of an Amazon girl
With hugs and kisses and arms wide open
I let you into my world
Now my feelings for you have been
shattered
Cracked,
Broken with seven years bad luck
Going through my mind are the words
"Love Sucks"

Still holding onto the memories and
dreams of what we could have been
Still trying to play it cool
Talking about "Let's be friends"
Acting all back on top, like you didn't hurt
me, like my heart didn't drop, my dreams
of independence didn't flop
You know I liked you, I liked you a lot,
maybe loved you but I can't be just friends
with you,
Not now, because I still feel like a fool for
losing myself in you

Last Monday

So, I saw my Ex today
"Girl, how have you been?"
I was lost for words to say,
Hmm, how have I been?
"You know it was my birthday last Monday
right?"
The idiot asked me
"Oh, it was"
I replied as I try to hide
my eyes full of non-surprise
"I guess you forgot?"
(Sigh, eyes roll behind his back
"Oh, yeah, I forgot," Jackass)
Now I could have simply said yes I forgot,
Forgot
Noooooooottttttt
I wasn't going to pretend I didn't
remember
But if I did I would have called
Wishing you birthday blessing,
Professing & confessing
Suggesting we be friends
After all, you only messed with my
emotions, what's that to a lifelong
friendship with a swell guy like you? (Eyes
roll)
"Actually, sweetie I knew"
I would've called you
But my former-love I didn't want to
Cause last Monday
You told me you loved me
Last Monday
You and I prayed for us

Last Monday
You made me laugh
Last Monday
You stole my heart
Then Last Monday
You tore us apart
Last Monday
You took back "I love you"
And replaced it with a deafening silence
Last Monday
I cried
My soul died for 59 seconds
Last Monday
I got over you
Last Monday
I finally knew what to do
Last Monday
I took care of me
Last Monday
Baby-girl, went on a shopping spree
"I'm sorry, did you say something?
Oh, that's right you grew up Last Monday"
"Anyway see yah!"
Sincerely Tisha

The Birth

Tonight another one was born
Because of you
You shook me up
And inspired me to write

My Name

Do it again
Say it again
Call my name again
Words more beautifully spoken
Has never left your lips
And collided with my ears
I like how you take your time with it
And let it roll off your tongue
Sometimes hearing my name from you
Makes me feel like my name is yours
It belongs to you
Say it again
Whisper those connecting letters in my
ears
And let my name flow through the air
Till it returns to me
Me, me, me, me, me

Confessions

They say absence make the heart grow
fonder
I never heard a statement more true
My confession is; oh, I miss you
God you linger in my mind like the words
on a stop sign
I'd rather go
But the orange light says go slow
I wait and I wait and I wait
For the light to turn green
But red is the only colour to be seen
So I stop
And then I remember again, how much I
miss you
Straining each voice that jumps in my
ears
Hoping once again I'd hear yours
And you would call my name
LATISHA
Okay, this is my confession
I am hoping and hoping and hoping
You would just.............
Come see me
One more time again

Energy

Wasting too much energy
Trying to pretend
That for you I don't have feelings
If I act like I am not trippin' over you
I'd be lying and that's something I just
can't do
Wasting too much energy trying to lie
Acting as though you are not the guy
Who got me caught, straight up trippin'
over you
That's something I just can't do
Too much energy
Trying not too miss you
But no not that
That's just something I can't do
I do, I do, I do
Miss and wish
I was with you

Last Name

I think I love you
But
I don't even know your last name
I think I love you
But
I don't even know the year you were
conceived
I think I love you
But
I have never met your parents
I think I love you
And
I want to spend the rest of our lives
Knowing you

Advice

Hope she's nice
Take my advice
Oh no
I think I want you
Now what?
 I sent you to her
Now what am I going to do?
Hope she's nice
You took my advice
Oh no
Now I want you
Instead

Good Sex

Good sex comes from within
When all minds are clear
Of everything except
The ones good sex is pursuing
Good sex knows how to touch
And where to touch too
Good sex is when the ambience is just
right
and its just us two
Good sex knows exactly what to do
It turns you on, then turns you out
Makes you scream, makes you shout
Good sex sticks the key in the ignition
And ignite fire
It takes you higher and higher into the
ecstasy
Of love
Driving fast, driving slow
Then stops when it reaches its destination
And both driver and passenger
Is satisfied
With Good Sex joy ride

If it's not about the sex

If it's not about the sex
Then why when I say no
You say goodbye
If it's not about the sex
Why when I shut you down
You suddenly don't have the time
If it's not about the sex
Then why when I pull your hand from
under my skirt
You act like a jerk
You pull away, you shut me out
You walk away and walk out
Then you want to convince me
 It's not sex you are about
Yeah right!

Honey

I think it's time you taste my honey
Packaged and labeled just for you
I got a bottle in my bedroom
Now tell me whatchu gonna do
If I let you come inside
Would you come alone?
Or would you bring your boys?
Would you talk about what you got?
Or would you keep less noise
I think it's time you taste my honey
Tell me, do you think you can handle it?
A bittersweet flava you never tasted before
It'll leave you yearning for more and more
I got to admit, it's the shit
After your first lick
You'll be an addict
I think it's time you taste my honey
But you got to know this boo
I don't share this honey with just anyone
I'm saving it for you
So if you are still trying new flavas and
dipping your fingers
In many honey bowls
You better slow your roll
Back off honey
Off my honey
I'm sealing my honey bowl

Average Joe

Johnny D he looked my way
Average Joe carried my books to school
Brad P winked his eye at me
Average Joe helped me with my homework
Steven S point at me and showed me to
his boys
Average Joe wrote me a poem
Van D walked over to me
Average Joe brought me roses
Vin D said, "Hello, Sexy"
Average Joe said, "Good Morning,
Beautiful"
Sylvester S said "Take a ride with me"
Average Joe asked, "Would you like to go
out with me?"
I said yes to Arnold Swat, I said no to
Average Joe
Tom C had his fun
Average Joe stayed alone
Freddie P Jr said Goodbye
Average Joe heard my cry
Leonardo D dated Halle
Average Joe dated me
Mel G dumped J.Lo
Average Joe and I got engaged
Beyonce killed Denzel
And I,
And me,
I am Mrs. Average Joe

Mood Ring

That was it for me, you know like the kind
of life defining moment
Like Jerry Mcguire's "you had me at hello"
When you put that ring on my finger,
I knew that cheap piece of plastic meant
more to me
Than the sand means to the sea
Most of the time it's hue reflected my
happy mood
This was the result of having you in my
life
But when it all change so quickly
My ring turned ugly too and this was also
because of you
Now the sadness has gone away and today
is a brand new day
Actually today's my birthday
I'm twenty-two and my new boo (love)
Has brought me a mood ring too
Now here is my dilemma if I let it be
Should I tell him, once before how much a
mood ring meant to me or should I let this
memory of my past with you haunt me
and cause me to affect all my relationships
anew
Should I let it go and love more than I
have ever love before
What should I do?

Tears on my Pillow

By the time you return
I'll be gone
I've just been waiting here for you too long
The pillows and sheets have absorb every
tear
I've cried all my cries in the name of you
Now I can no longer stay here
There's nothing else I can do
But wipe my tears away
The tears on the pillow
Are the broken pieces of you and me
It's the end of us

The Stupidest Thing

I done-done it
I've done the stupidest thing
I let you play me for a fool
I just should have trust my guts
Which told me keep it simple stupid
Stay away
Don't fall
I knew better and what did I do
I lied to myself too

Good Bye

If this is not Goodbye
Then why is my heart
Shedding tears tonight

If this is not Goodbye
Then why does my body feel so numb

If this is not Goodbye
Why do my fingers
Tremble at your touch

If this is not Goodbye
Then tell me why is it I miss you so much

If this is not Goodbye
Then why does my body yearn for your
warmth

If this is not Goodbye
Why as our lips touch
It is as if it is our last kiss

If this is not Goodbye
Then why is my body crying out for you
If this is not Goodbye

Faze

One time, quite a time ago
You looked at me like you were in love
Almost in love but not quite in love

I trusted you with my delicate heart
Hoping you weren't what the obvious
stated
Hoping you wouldn't disappoint me or
hurt me

But more time went by in our phenomenal
affair
And it seemed you got bored of me or
something
Because you stopped calling me

Now I see you around time after time
You'll ask me the strangest questions like
"Why I stopped calling you?" or
"Why I broke YOUR heart?"

Boy seriously I think your crazy
No sorry, stupid
I didn't break your heart I loved you with
all my heart
But I was just a faze to you

So you see me around looking my usual
Bootilicious way
Then you want a hug and a kiss and
another hug

Here we go again
"Girl, why you stop calling me?" you'd say
And then I'd have to reply
"aaaaahhhhh, I don't know, maybe I'm
sick of being just a faze you go through"

Child, when you want me for real, for
always, you can call me
Actually, no screw that, you lost your
chance, never call me again

DejaVu

I am willing to try to open up to you
But something just keeps holding me back
It seems this is like dejavu
Whenever I am with you

I've been here many times before
Only with different faces
I have heard these sweet nothings before,
wondering if you really mean this

It's wonderful you feel comfortable
I'm glad you're willing to trust your heart
with me
I'm happy you offer me eternity

But I feel as though I have heard this
already
Promises of commitment & security
How can my heart feel secure?
When a hundred times these same
promises were made to me before

I use to think taking risk is what loves
about
Now risk after risk is wearing me out
I'm tired, frustrated of giving out chances
To those who are not worthy, then to lose
So once again I'm taking a chance with
you the one I choose
If I end up broken hearted
You are the one to blame
I will let you through
In hopes you won't be the same

A Poem 4 u

You ask me why I stopped smiling with
you
I don't call u as often as I use to
In fact, I barely call u

It's simple the reasons why
When I call u
Ur never there
When u speak
Ur not sincere

When I touch u
U pull away
You promise you'll come over
And you don't do what you say

You ask me if I miss you
But apparently you don't miss me
Putting up with this is utter misery

You want to own me, control me
But you don't want to be there for me

You take all my kindness, my love and set
it aside like an antique
Holding it near but not holding it dear

You don't kiss me, touch me, hug me, and
hold me
You don't go out with me, you don't
introduce me as your lady, I'm just a girl u
like secretly

In fact, you basically hide me
You want to bury me like a bone of a dog,
 to return to me later
When no one's looking, like I'm nothing
That's how you my dear make me feel
Like nothing
Just an image, a voice you constantly hear
and see
A heart you can trample on easily

I never really wanted much from you
I just wanted you to love me with all that I
am
But of course that proved to be easier said
than done

But I am definitely not nothing
I am a rose, I am sunshine, I am a
shooting star,
Didn't you know?
I am the leaves in the spring, the heat in
summer and winter's snow

I'm beautiful on the inside and out
Sorry you're too blind to see or to stupid to
act on the opportunity

Anyway, I can't take it
This illusion known as you and me
Now when I think of you it just depresses
me

So I 'm not down with it
I'm not having it
And I'm certainly not feeling it

Either you got to go
or I got to go boo
I despise u
I no longer long to be with you
You wanted me to write a
poem 4 u
Well, how do u like it now?

Broken Promises

Broken promises
Are broken trust
If you can't keep your word
I can't believe in us

Why say you'll do it
If you never had any intensions to
Broken promises are reflections of you

You are undependable
You're just a waste of my time
You say one thing
Then do nothing messing with my mind

It's really too bad you can't keep your
word

Hit and Run
(I am sorry for my tongue, but I was hurt)

Why does it not surprise me?
 You don't call me anymore
Why is this not a shock?
You must think I'm a whore

Just another player in your little game
You probably don't even remember my
name
I honestly thought you were different
But all you wanted was my c@%t

I thought you wanted the real me
Now the truth I see
You never cared, not at all
It's been two weeks and you still haven't
called

I spoke to a friend of yours last night too
He said "the truth is he never liked you"
I should have known from the start
I wished I never gave you my heart

I'm okay, it's all good
I still love the same
Your game is totally understood
You hurt me a lot
But I'll make it through
So my dear sweet lover
F@%k you

I hope you had a good time
I hope you had fun

You're just another loser
Just another hit and run.

Anger

It was anger that made you step up to me
Yell at me and try to hurt me

It was anger that made you put your
hands around my neck
And squeeze as tight as you could

It was anger that made you not answer
when I call
It made you do those horrible things after
all

It made you isolate yourself from the ones
you love
Shut them out and put up a wall

It was anger the spawn your jealousy
It was this that made you try to hurt me
It is Satan who designed anger
The anger which infest
It's way into you and me

It's Anger
It's Satan
It is you
It is me

I'll Make It

You had me where you wanted me for long
enough
Now that it's over I got to be tough
I must admit you really did me wrong
But now that you're gone I will be strong

It took me a while to walk away
But now I am out of the game, you are out
of my way
You lied to me, you used me
You did what you had to do

I'm not taking it anymore
I am not putting up with you
I did my best for you
You treated me like trash

So don't think I won't live right without
you
Cause I'll live it up
Don't think I won't see without you
Cause I'll keep looking up
Don't think I won't hear without you
I hear the rhythm of the beat
Don't think I won't dance without you
Cause the groove I will seek

Don't think I won't love without you
Because my heart is full
I will live, I will love, I will breathe
I will hug, I will kiss, I will dream
I will feel, I will scream
I will make it

Brotha Man, Brotha Man

Brotha Man, Brotha Man
When are you gonna stop playing baby
boy
Posing off with that girl like she is a
collector's toy

Brotha Man, Brotha Man
When are you gonna do all you can
To start acting like a real man

Brotha man, Brotha Man
Put that damn P.S.2 down
Turn your good for nothing
Scrub's life around

It's time to stop tease her
Step off that played out track
And please her
Stop copping out and shopping out
Get off your ass and take her out

Her body is a wonderland

And he doesn't know it
Girlfriend it isn't your responsibility to
show it
Let that man use his eyes
And see
Whatshu got, your beauty

Buying her diamonds and things
Bracelet and rings
That's not a crime

The crime is
Not giving that angel your time
of day

Take time to know her
Then you show her you care
You are aware
That she is an angel
But not in disguise
It's obvious
To every fool but you

Then do what you got to do
To make it right
Grab her by the hand
And fight
To keep her in your life

That girl is mine
That girl is mine

I am a man
And I know what a girl wants

She wants me

Bare naked: what if it was your mother?

Have you ever loved a woman?
Ok, Ok
I know you're tired of this
But just give me a minute of your time
 to flow with this
Excuse me for stating the obvious
do you know what she is?
She is a female
A woman, a girl
A senorita, a lady, a sista
I know your vision might be a little fuzzy
right now
Cause all you can see is the mini skirts
Tall boots, big boobs
Fine ass booty
If she was naked
You would see naked
Not beauty
There she is bare naked
Baring her soul to you
And what do you do?
What do you do?
You rip the clothes off her
Bare naked skin
And rape her
Sure she said yes
It was consensual
But when she said I love you
And you said it back knowing full well
When the sex was done
You were done
You were being hypocritical
A rapist, stealing her belief in love

Leaving her to take a cold shower
To wash off the pain, anguish and sorrow
Images of a lost tomorrow
Imprinted in her skin
Kiss after kiss
Bite after bite
Hicky after hicky
Ahhh and ooohh
And goodnight
Goodbye, so called love
The "I love you"
You are so beautiful, then the blues
Was I really beautiful?
Or did he find a way to get in?
Why did he go?
Why did he go?
He's the ho
No, he's the man
Doesn't matter he shattered my heart
I'm a woman, I should know better
Now all I have left is second hand,
third hand
4th, 5th, 8th, 10th
on and on and on
I mean second hand goods
Imagine if some guy did what you did to
me
To your mother, your sister, your aunty
What would you do?
Would you still have done it to me?

Chapter Five
"War"

This Chapter talks about all kinds of wars, internal wars, political wars, office wars, people wars, personal wars and bloody wars.

Rage against War

Bright eyes
Eyes of innocence
Not yet to know the world that is their
reality
Where man follows man
And fight and kill unnecessary
What have you done to deserve death
before life?
Is it you to blame for cruelty
Collateral damage, that's what you be
Just another casualty
Bright eyes, tears
Drops of salty sadness
Holding on so tightly
On to he the rock of their security
"Daddy, don't go, Daddy"
if he wants a fight so badly, why doesn't
he alone, go out and fight
Call me naive but I fail to see how
a get them before they get us mentality
is right, but just think WHAT IF they never
intended to get you
Hold up, I said WHAT IF
Than how can your reason for all this
blood-shed be justified?
You don't know me; I live in a little rock by
the sea
But I too, we too will pay for your decision
We too will suffer the consequences
So how can they be any winners, any
problems resolved by
Bombs after bombs, death of innocent
men, women, children

People will go hungry because of you
People will die because of you
Mr. Earthly Man-in-Charge, can't you hear
your people crying out to you
No hate, no war, no weapons of mass
destruction
So tonight I call out to all my brothers and
sisters
Get down on bended knee
And pray to HE
So our people will find hope in the midst
of evil
I don't know who's wrong or right
And I don't care
You are a man acting as a God
And anyone who murders people
People for any cause is still a monster
Not a hero
When it's over with so many dead, so
many tears, traumas and fears
What have we accomplished, does
everything suddenly become alright
Do we make the world a better place?
When you look at your adversary
Do you not see your own reflection
steering back at you?
Start with your own, protect your own
Stop trying to dominate and negotiate
Stop the killing
It isn't you that's dying
It isn't you leaving your kids behind
Look in the mirror, tell me what you see
 Then ask yourself
What world are you creating for your
Children's children

War within

Our young people are fighting a war
Not many know what they are fighting for
Some don't even know their enemies from
friends
Just keeping all defenses up until the war
meets
its end
Some fight for their country
Some their family
Some fight to keep their pride
Guns, knives, words of hate
Weapons of destruction
Our young soldiers fight
But against what
The war within
The battle for their souls
The most difficult war to fight

Some People

They are some people who really give you
a hard time
Waiting for your walls to come down so
they can do the crime

They will come to you and take a bite out
of your skin
Sit there and steer at you
Waiting for you to do the wrong thing

Searching for every single flaw
From what you say or wear
They even talk about how you do your hair

And it seems as if all their energy
Is focused on you
They just sit there and wait
Inspecting everything you do

They search your trash
Tap your phones
Looking for incriminating news

Evidence which confirm their theories
Oops, you're human too
I've discovered
When you cut her she bleeds
Onions make her eyes water
A funny joke triggers her laughter

They are some pots
Oops, I mean people
Waiting to sell you out

Call the kettle black
They are some people
Just out to get you
No matter what

Collateral Damage

Am I really that invisible to you?
Am I not a woman?
Do I not have eyes?
Just like you
Do I not sweat?
Just like you
You say you care
You promised me freedom
You lied
How can I be free?
When I am not the girl
I use to be
This face
This is not mind
I am tarnished
No man will take me for his wife
I am not beautiful
I am scarred
No one will ever make love to me
And do you care
You do not know me
I am nothing but a dot in your big picture
But do I not laugh?
Just like you
Do I not cry?
Just like you
But my tears just fall
And are lost in the streets filled with red
Puddles of blood
And lifeless bodies
But do you care
You promised us freedom
But all I see is death

Death surrounds me
Till it becomes all I know
You promised freedom
But I have lost it all

Woman's Pill

Now I am coming into my own
I find myself even more lost and confused
Now that I know what I want
I find myself facing my destiny alone

Now that I see the world for what it truly is
I find myself crying a lot more
Now that I know I have to fight
I find myself weak in the knees

Now that I know who I am
I find myself begging the ones I love
"pleaaaaaaaaaaaasssssssssssssse, release
me, let me go?"

And let me be me, free me
Some people judge you based on who you
use to be
Try to understand, the old me is gone

Even when I think I've won
I still lost, I lose you
Because you make me feel as though I
have to
Choose who...

Me or who you'd like me to be
Because I have not succeeded by
definition of
Man's standards
I am a failure to you

Sure I've grown internally

Does that matter to you?
These things you don't see

I'm trying to go after my dreams
Why do you have to be the one I have to
fight
for my right to reach the top
why won't you just shut up
Just stop

Listen

So I am steering in the mirror
At my own reflection
And start to think about how
I am alone in my room right now
And I am holding a bottle of women's pills
And I am contemplating this fact
If I took a whole bunch, I have a hunch
No one would be around to notice that

When they came home
I would be gone
And they would all wish I'd come back

So I look to the left
Then looked to the right
In one hand the pills
In the other my pen and paper

And I thought to myself
What should I do?
I prayed to God
And he directed me to write
So I write with all my might

Sometimes

Sometimes I sit alone and just shed tears
Wondering why I was born in this time
A time when one has so many fears

I see the newspaper day by day
All there's left for me to do is pray
They're shooting, stabbing, killing for no
reason
Without a second thought or care

Everyday you walk the roads in fear
What if I look at someone too hard?
Or accidentally step on one's toe

Will they kill me, will they shoot me
I just don't know
A simple "I'm sorry" doesn't mean
anything anymore

"That's okay, it happens"
Isn't said now, like it was before
Father in heaven to you I pray
Continue to protect me from the evil
around me day by day

The Tattoo Thing

Taught I would be different
If I brand my skin
Taught they'd see a unique one
If I do the tattoo thing

So I went to the parlor
had it done
I mean, life is for the living
This should be fun

Taught when it was over
It'll all be cool
Shoot, after I did it
I felt like a fool

Is this the kind of person I want to be?
Tattoo one, tattoo two, tattoo three
Now the world's got a label on me

Instead of an artist
I'm a punk
Instead of a leader
I am a trouble-maker
Labels
I'm one of those who spoiled my skin
Not one comfortable in the skin I'm in

Not ready for you to judge me
Before you know me
Not ready to be one of "them"
Instead of me

The Truth

Damn the bigger man with the power in
his hands
The unfair bully who rules the majority
Because of his financial security

Damn the unjust employer
Who seeks profit at the expense of others
suffering

The truth they seek to hide at these so-
called executive meetings
Where they discuss the future, our future

Where they discuss the future of their
bank accounts
and it's increase

They don't care about us
We mean less to them than the rocks on
the bottom of their aquariums, where their
beautiful priceless fish, which'll never be
someone's Sunday dish, live

The deceit, the lies they tell,
So we will work till our hands swell
Work hard as hell

They cover up the truth
Truth is no company is anything without
the sweaty hands of the common man

No neighborhood is germ-free without
the garbage collector to do his duty

We are all significant; we all have our role
to play
Money does not define us
Today is our day

Revolution From Within

It's true no one can make you feel
inferior if you don't want to
You can be shackled in chains,
hands and feet
And still not suffer defeat
You are as free as you want to be

Sometimes our mind keeps us blind
Prisoners inside our heads
You are powerful, you are strong,
Only to be weakened by what you think
wrong

People try to control you by calling out
your sins
But let the man without sin cast the first
stone
The revolution comes from within

Decide in your mind
I am free
And no man on this earth has control of
me
I am strong
I will do no wrong
I am wise
And demons I despise
I am a child of God

I have the right to fight
For my place next to the King
The revolution comes from within

No Respect

Never did anything to you to deserve such
lack of RESPECT

Obviously I offended you because for me
you have no RESPECT

Running out of patience for your absence
of RESPECT

Every man deserves RESPECT

So from you I demand your RESPECT

Please, Thank you, Good Morning,
Goodnight in affect

Everyone of God's creatures deserve
RESPECT

Can you offer me your RESPECT?

To you I give my RESPECT

PMS

Blame it on PMS
Why I act the way I do
Call it what you like
But don't blame it on you

The one who brings my moodiness out
The tears, the cussing, the yelling
The urge to scream and shout

Blame it on PMS
Why I can be such a Bitch
But don't say you're the one making me
switch

Cause I'm telling you
It's PMS

Billing Clerk

5: 00 A.M
The alarm goes off
Beap-beap-beap-beap
Bang, I bust it in two
I get up iron my shirt
Have breakfast
Take a shower
Catch the bus
Now, I am here
Where the silence is deafening
Only to be broken by the constant ringing
of
telephones and the printing of printers
Lord knows the printing
Riiiiiiiiiinnnnnnnngggggggg
"Hello, how may I help you?"
"Yes, dear, I would like to make an order
please"
The minutes go by
Now I got to go
Not home yet, to the bathroom
Guess what, I have to ask permission
Laughable but true
"Excuse me Miss Supervisor; I'm going to
the bathroom,"
The walls are closing in
The same walls I see day out and day in
The familiar walls over and over again
I want to scream
"Ahhhhhhhhhhh"
I scream
Just breathe.......Aaaaahhh

Lord why do you punish me
What did I do to deserve such monotony?
Back at my desk the computer is a blur
The words are fading, I am losing my
sanity
Is that a D or a C, an A or an R?
I want to shout
"Arrrrrrgh"
Just Breathe.....Ahhhh
Relax

11:59 A.M
tick-tock, tick-tock
tick-tock
Lunch
Got to rush, Got to go
I'll eat on the way
Got so many bills to pay
In a hour

1:05 P.M
I'm late, again
Fax, Fax, Fax and more fax
But I'm so tired
YAWN
I think I need a cure
Because I caught me a case of niggeritus

4:29 P.M
tick-tock, tick-tock
School's out
Oops, I mean
It's time to go
Now I'll exhale and take it slow

In my ride, I pass the ocean and gaze at
the scenery
I inhale the fresh air
And just relax

Sing: I feel good, tan na na na na, I knew
that would now
Home at last, home at last
Ate ham and bread and some fruit
Hit the beach, went for a jog
Return home, turn on the radio
Listen to some Kenny G
Calmed my reality
Dance, Dance, Dance
Wrote a poem,
With scented candles all around I soaked
in a tub
filled with rose petals and lavender bubble
bath
Exhale and Relax

4: 49 P.M
Latisha
Latisha
Latisha

Wake up, girl
"hunh, hunh, what?"

You were daydreaming again, aren't you
going home?

"What do you mean, I thought I was
home"

In my real ride, I am dozing off because
I'm exhausted
In the Minivan stand waiting on a second
van to go home
It still hasn't arrived yet
The rain start to fall
Don't have my umbrella
Take cover

6:00 P.M
Just got a van
6:30 P.M
Just got home

Dirty dishes, unswept floor
And I am hungry
But tired so I'll just rest for a bit

8: 45 P.M
Wash dishes, sweep floor
It's time to cook?
 I really don't think so
I'll drink a cup of tea and go to bed hungry

No, wait, not this
REWIND
5:00 A.M
Alarm goes off
I take a deep breath, kneel down and pray
I ask God to take care of me today
Cold shower...morning jazz on my radio
And I go
Take the world by storm with God at my
right hand

Sing: His eyes are on the sparrow and I
know he watches me

PAY DAY-Month End
Phone bill, light bill, more bills
I wanna scream but wait not today
Today I sing

"Oh happy day, oh happy day
that Jesus wash, wash my sins a way"

Then I do it all again.

Slit My Wrist

Ssshhhhh
Cry no more for me
For I have chosen my own destiny
Blood, Pain, Agony

Took a knife and sliced another part of me
The passion that flowed through my veins
Drove me mad, destructively insane

When I was told, convinced to settle
To stay stagnant, stable, immobile
Secure
Get paid
So I stayed and I got paid
But my bills were too high
Aside from rent money, phone money,
utilities
It cost me my heart, my soul, my abilities

To think innovatively
To live creatively
To be expressive and poetic
To live flow-etic
A rose in a glass case fading away
Once a beauty to behold in Mother
Nature's garden

Just left to be observed till she died and
after her death, they asked why
A prisoner of her life
They wondered why she took that knife
Slit her wrist and took her life
But she was already dead

They didn't know
When they took her out of the field
And put her in a cozy office instead
Blood, Pain, Agony
Pressure to be who she never wanted to be
All she wanted was to be heard
To spread her word
To make a difference, help someone
To save a life
But who was going to save her
From herself, from hell
From the MAN
Who convinced us all
It is just silly to dream bigger than
"Good Day Sir, how may I direct your
call?"
"Yes Sir, Please hold"

Don't they know that I have a dream that
one day...
My dreams will come true
Martin Luther King Jr, he had a dream
Nelson Mandela, he had a dream
Errol Walton Barrow, he had a dream
Bussa, he had a dream
Rosa Parks, she had a dream

Must I sit here and die inside
Let my dreams cry inside
Until I'm brought back to life by another
life

I choose to dream, to live but if I stay still
On a count of you
Death will be my only alternative

Suicide my only option
To rescue me from this agony
of placing an artist in an office

Blood, Pain, Agony
I just wanna say
Mummy, I love you
Good Bye World

Who are Errol Walton Barrow and Bussa?

*These are Barbadian (Barbados) National
Heroes. To find out more about them and
Barbados, log on to www.barbados.gov.bb.*

Snake

You glide around in the green-green grass
I can't see you, you're camouflaged
I know you're there
So why don't you come out?
You think you've got me figured out?
You smile at me face to face
Then I turn my back
And you bite me without haste
You are my friend you made me believe
But all the time, it's me you deceive
Stop messing with my mind
Stop messing with my head
What is it you want?
Do you want me alive or dead?
Can I trust you?
I think not
You are a snake
And now you're caught

Afraid

I'm afraid to live
I'm afraid to shout
I'm afraid to smile
I'm afraid to cry
I'm afraid to hurt
I'm afraid of being hurt
I'm afraid to love
I'm afraid to hate
I'm afraid to move on
I'm afraid to wait
I'm afraid of heaven
I'm afraid of hell
I'm afraid to touch
I'm afraid to smell
I'm afraid of me
I'm afraid of you
I'm too afraid of life
Tell me what to do?

Disappointment of man

I hate too much attention
I hate to be ignored
I hate to be judge or accused
I hate to be cheated or used

I hate not getting my credit due
I hate when you're watching everything I
do
I hate when you act like you don't care
about me
I hate when you don't see what you should
see

I hate how ignorance is rewarded
I hate how integrity has been demoted
I hate how excellence has lowered the bar
Who the hell do you think you are?
I hate the impossible standards you set for
me
I hate being judge because of my amount
of money
I hate the lighter the skin the prettier I am
These are some of the disappointments of
man

Chapter Six
"Under My Christmas Tree"

This Chapter talks about my most favorite time of the year Christmas, the birth and death of Jesus Christ, the true meaning of Christmas, the thankfulness of Christmas and the spirit of Christmas

De Sweetest Kinda Kandy Kane

This is Christmas
Happiness and joy floats through the air
This is Christmas
And there are smiling faces everywhere
But this Christmas
My heart is sad and blue
Cause this Christmas
This Christmas there's no you

This is Christmas
I'm glad my family is here
This is Christmas
I'm blessed to have a family that cares
But this Christmas
When I look under the tree
I will be disappointed
Unless God sends you to me

This is Christmas
It's about sharing special things
I love Christmas
And the kindness that it brings
But this Christmas
There is a gift I simply must give
This Christmas
For you awaits a mistletoe kiss

And if you think that was special
Just wait
There's more too
This is Christmas
My heart, my body, my soul
I give to you

This Christmas
Unless you hold me tight
There's not a damn thing on this earth
That will make this Christmas feel right
So thank goodness this Christmas you are
still my boo
Thank goodness this Christmas
I still got you; to hug, hold, and kiss under
the mistletoe
To share my heart's deepest desires with

This Christmas
The sweetest gift to me
Is to share it with you
And to have you next to me

Why we celebrate

Happy Birthday
2 u
Dear Jesus
This Christmas
I promise not to 4get
Why we celebrate
Because you were born
2 die so we can live
And until blood stops flowing through my
veins
I will keep Christmas in my heart
Happy Birthday 2 u

Hurry Up!

Hurry up
Hurry up
Christmas is soon here
Hurry up
Hurry up
Or get out our way
Hurry up
Hurry up
There's too much to do
Hurry up
Hurry up
I don't care about you
Hurry up
Hurry up
The church bells are ringing
Hurry up
Hurry up
The people are singing
Hurry up
Hurry up
Rush Christmas away
So we all can get back to a nicer day

Friends

As we sat at the Karaoke machine
Tara wanted to sing "Santa Baby"
Stacia wanted to sing
"Grandma, got run over by a reindeer"
and me I wanted to sing
"Rockin around the Christmas Tree"
We tried and we tried
But we couldn't agree

Time was a ticking
We kept on calling
Songs one by one
But couldn't decide,
No matter how hard we tried
This called for a compromise

I was getting a little upset
Cause nothing was going my way
Almost didn't even sing that day

But I thought no forget it
That's not what I should do
So we sang "Santa Baby"
And had a good time too

I got the feeling whether
It be "Rockin around the tree"
Or "Jingle Bell Rock"
Just having friends to sing with
The fun will never stop

On Strike!!!

Hey, listen up
I am on strike

No cooking
No housework
No nothing tonight

Listen Up!
I am on strike
Christmas hustle and bustle
Aint seeing me tonight

Tonight's the night
It's only me and you
Tonight's the night
And this is what I'll do

I'll slip into sexy
That clings to my body
I'll do my nails, fix my hair
Clean up nicely

Here open this
It's a gift just for me-
I mean you
Silk boxers, you like 'um
They'll look lovely
On you

Hey, listen up!
The candles are lit
Nat King Cole's on the player
Can you handle me-I mean it?

Hey, listen up!
Hold me tight
Because the only
Christmas I see is you here with me
And mistletoe tonight

Christmas Blues

Whatever it is
That's got you sad and blue
Don't cry, don't sob
Cause I'm here 4 u
Whatever it is
Making you cry
I'm here, I'm here
No need to ask why
Whatever it is
Whatever you do
Don't worry
I'll be here
I'll be here
With you

Relax

Relax
Breathe in
Breathe out
Don't forget what it's really about
Ssssshhhh
Calm down, don't shout
Remember what it is really about
If it's not fun
If you don't enjoy
Forget it
Don't employ
Relax
Breathe in
Breathe out
Don't forget what it's really about
Relax and just have
A very Merry
Christmas

Under my Christmas tree

Under my Christmas tree
Awaits a special gift for me
Somebody above must really love me

They must've heard me laugh
Sometimes heard me cry
They must've seen me smile
They must've seen me sigh

They knew what I desired
And rendered that gift to me

That special gift
Perfectly wrapped
Beneath my Christmas tree

I did not take a peek
But I surely know
What it would be

Someone oh someone
Must surely love me
They listen when I ask
They heard my heart shout

For the giver of this Christmas gift
Must know what I am about

So I finally took a look
I finally took a peek
As I suspected
It's the Christmas gift I seek

Not a Barbie Doll
A mansion on the hill
A diamond ring

This Christmas gift came
complete with everything

Family, joy, happiness, love
Peace and good friends
It even came with a wonderful
 Daughter and Husband

One by one
I counted what this entire gift
contained

And to make it
Very simple
I'll call the gift by name

Under my tree
Beneath the trimmings and wrappings
Was a present full of God's blessings

Destined to be King

Jesus,
Jesus,
Jesus,

Radiance of truth
An aroma of faith
Small little fingers
Mary held his hand as best
her weakened body could
So fragile
But yet she felt the strength
of a King
The strong-force that protected her son

"Destined to be King"
This was the cry of many,
 whom did not know the mother
Yet awaited the Son

Though she knew his time on this earth
would be short
And his stay by her side shorter still
She could not help feeling instantly
overprotective
of this boy

A boy with so much wisdom
Confidence, Faith and Love in his heart
Other boys his age could not comprehend
Destined to be more than just a
carpenters Son

She feared for him

Jesus,
My handsome boy
Jesus,
Oh, how I wish I could understand
What is your heavenly Father's plan?
Why send you to me?
To take you away again
Oh, how I wish I could understand

She dreaded yet expected the day when
her boy was to be a man and take his
thrown
as King

That day came, he left her home seeking
answers; she prayed to the Father "Why
must I let him go, I carried him, cared for
him, thought him all I know

My dear sweet
Mary, my virgin, Mary
Can't u see?
I have a plan for him
I have a plan for you

Trust me my Child
That boy, that man is
Destined to be king

Mary wiped her tears
Swallowed her fears
Then I must go to him
She took her sons
Her other sons
And went to seek him

"My mother and brothers,
who are my mother and brothers,
you are my mother,
you are my brother,
for whoever does the will of God,
that is the place of he"

"My God, my son has forsaken me"

"No my child, you have done your part,
gave him his start, remember now, a
Son's love
 for his mother, he will always have in his
heart,
But his journey must take its course

The words sang soundly on her ears
The vision of her little boy swam in her
tears

With every lash
And every cry

Mary sobbed,
Jesus, my boy

One Lash,
Jealousy

Another,
Racism

Another,
Hypocrisy

Another,
Poverty

Another,
Greed

Another,
Lust

Gluttony, Anger, Hate, Vanity
Impurity, Adultery, Murder

Lash after Lash
Nailed to the cross
Bearing a crown made of thorns
Cursed and persecuted
He died for our sins

Mary wept blood, as
her son bled
"Father, is this your plan all along?"

"This is for you, this is for my people
I give you my Son, so you may live"

"Forgive them Father,
for they know not what they do"

"My Lord, are you truly the Son of God,
why do you pray for them, after what
they've done to you?, if you are the Son of
God, save yourself"

Miracles

An aurora of light, a silent night
A visit from God's angel
An untouched woman, untouched by man
Was told she would see a miracle

The birth of a son
A wondrous one
He would change the world for everyone

The lord our God saw a world filled with
sin
So unto us he sent his son to save us from
suffering

A world of war, a world of hate
A world where man worship silver and
gold
So unto us he sent his son, the messiah to
behold

We live today
Because a boy became a man
He taught us good things,
Spoke of the lord our king

In this time we still see miracles
happening everyday
So open your eyes and be aware of God's
miracles I say

Chapter Seven
"The Sweetest Love"

This Chapter talks about when God brings two people together, true love, happiness, the love of God and art.

The Story of Us

What made me stay?
When I was suppose to go
I don't know

But when I saw you
I knew
I had to know you

And in your eyes I did see
You, yourself needed to know me

What made me stay and watch?
Instead of leave
Beats me

But when our eyes locked
And I spoke to you without
Opening my mouth

I knew that day
There was something about u
Little did I knew
I had no clue
The story of us
Would begin with you
And go like this.....

I'm shock
I can not believe
The evolution of this thing
Evolving to the day you would
Give me a ring

Professing, confessing
A love-marriage-eternity
thing
Man, I never knew
Not once had a clue

That this soft silhouette
Under the sunset
Would one day be more than
Just a crush

But really a real u and me
A real us

I wanted it, yes
From that moment
We exchange numbers

I wanted you to be the husband
I envisage God made for me

Though never in my wildest dreams
Did I see
This reality

Every single time I look at you
I'm amazed
We're finally here
After all we went through

And you know my favorite part?
Every day we add a new page of passion,
mystery and love
And this story's yet to end

Spend my Life

Because of who you are
When I talk to God
I shake his hand
I kiss his feet
I wrap my arms around him
And thank him for his son
Because of who you are
I praise my father
"Yes, I have finally found someone"
Someone I have prayed for since I was a
teenager
A support system, a friend, a lover
I couldn't complain or ask for another
I just want to spend my life with you
Forever

The Sweetest Love

I'm on bending knee
God, you are so good to me
I'm standing on my heels
I'm dancing on my toes
I'm singing with my eyes
I'm screaming with my nose
If no one else here gets me
That's okay, you do
You understand and love me endlessly
You wouldn't try to change me
You only want to teach me
To be the best at whom I am and what I do
To be the best me
L.J.G.B
A gem
The sweetest love I'll ever know
Lord you are worthy of all my praise

Art

Art awakens life in many ways, influences
many feelings
Inspires many dreams

Art has many forms, textures and colors
Is presented in many ways
Art goes beyond the artist's eyes
It is meant to be admired

Art follows no rules, maintains no
standards
Governed by no law, has no formula, no
system
It is freedom of expression

Art is united among races, faces, colors,
cultures, languages
We are all capable of being art and
appreciating art
Art is not what it is but what we want it to
be

An artist is nothing without a subject
Open your eyes and see art is all around

Happy

Not another song of sadness
Not another word of pain
No more rhymes of anger
No more speeches of hate

Can't hear anymore
Won't listen to you
I can't take your baggage
I won't feel your pain

For I am love
The purest you'll ever know
You can't hurt me anymore
As long as there is a God above

I am surrounded by love
The purest you'll ever know
I can't carry your baggage anymore

For I am young
I am free
Free from the world's insanity

Too many good things in this life
For me to focus on chaos and strife
Too much to love, not enough to hate
You can not, shall not banish me to your
miserable state

I am and always will be
Happy

My God

I cried
He wiped my tears
I screamed
He heard my fears
I fell to my knees
He picked me up
I spilled my water
He refilled my cup
I closed my heart
He opened it up
I lost my will
He found it and gave it back
I was alone
He stayed with me
I was cold
He put his loving arm around me
I was going too fast
He slowed me down
I was a fool
He gave me wisdom
So who do I love unconditionally?
No matter what, who is always there for
me?
HE
MY GOD
HIM

I am

I am an artist, I am a musician
I am a writer, I am a speaker
I am a hero, I am a king
I am a queen, I am everything

I listen when my people speak
I listen when the birds sing
I hear your prayers
I see your tears
Cause I am everything

I see your smiles, I hear your laughter
I am your negotiator
I am your warrior

I am a soldier, I am a leader
I am a movie star, I am a house keeper
I am the clouds in the sky
I am the heaven, I am the earth
I am death, I am birth

If you ask it will be given to you
Just wait on me my people
Your prayers are heard and will be
answered
You'll see
I listen when you speak to me
But all good things take time
Don't panic, don't worry
Don't feel alone
Just let your bright light shine
You're not forgotten
I am a fighter, I am your champion

Beautiful Blessings

Beautiful Blessings are the moments we
share
Beautiful Blessings are the ones who care
Beautiful Blessings are the ones we love
Beautiful Blessings comes from above
Beautiful Blessings are beautiful smiles
Beautiful Blessings are laughter for miles
Beautiful Blessings are kisses and hugs
Beautiful Blessings are lots of love
Beautiful Blessings are the things we do
Beautiful Blessings are moments with you

A New Beginning

Every year is a new adventure
Till my days are done
Every day a new experience
The bad days and good ones

Every mistake is a chance of a fresh start
Every misdemeanor a chance for a change
of heart
So this year is coming to an end but not
the memories
of what we did and making new friends

So ring in the new year with great pride
and joy
No regrets, just lessons learnt
New philosophies and respect earned

It's time for you to start praising
Praise the lord
For a new beginning

About the Author

Born in Barbados, an island in the Caribbean of a Barbadian (Barbados) mother and a Vincentian (St. Vincent and the Grenadines) father; Latisha, age twenty-five, has been falling in love with the art of poetic expression for the last seven years. Taking an active interest in the literary arts in her country, she has pursued many projects in the field. During this time, she used this forum to channel her feelings towards many experiences of her youth. In 2005, her life changed completely when she married and a year later gave birth to her first born. The poems illustrated in this book tell the story of a teenage girl growing into a young woman. These are poems based on real emotions and experiences and document a life journey through adolescence to womanhood. However, the story continues as this woman becomes a wife and a mother and experiences a whole new world of emotions.

"Ask and it will be given to you; seek and you will find; knock and the door will be opened to you. For everyone who asks receives; he who seeks finds; and to him who knocks, the door will be opened."

Matthew 7:7-8

www.ingramcontent.com/pod-product-compliance
Lightning Source LLC
Chambersburg PA
CBHW031956040426
42448CB00006B/386